GRANNY TORRELLI M

by
Sharon Creech

Student Packet

Written by
Sharan Farmer

Contains masters for:

2 Prereading Activities
6 Vocabulary Activities
1 Study Guide
3 Character Analysis Activities
2 Critical Thinking Activities
2 Literary Analysis Activities
3 Quizzes
1 Novel Test

PLUS Detailed Answer Key
and Scoring Rubric

Teacher Note

Selected activities, quizzes, and test questions in this Novel Units® Student Packet are labeled with the appropriate reading/language arts skills for quick reference. These skills can be found above quiz/test questions or sections and in the activity headings.

Note

The 2005 Harper Trophy paperback edition of the book, © 2003 by Sharon Creech, was used to prepare this guide. The page references may differ in other editions. Novel ISBN: 0-06-440960-0

Please note: Please assess the appropriateness of this book for the age level and maturity of your students prior to reading and discussing it with them.

ISBN 978-1-60539-021-5

Printed in the United States of America.

To order, contact your local school supply store, or—

Novel Units, Inc.
P.O. Box 97
Bulverde, TX 78163-0097

Web site: www.novelunits.com

Note to the Teacher

Selected activities, quizzes, and test questions in this Novel Units® Student Packet are labeled with the following reading/language arts skills for quick reference. These skills can be found above quiz/test questions or sections and in the activity headings.

Basic Understanding: The student will demonstrate a basic understanding of written texts. The student will:

- use a text's structure or other sources to locate and recall information (Locate Information)
- determine main idea and identify relevant facts and details (Main Idea and Details)
- use prior knowledge and experience to comprehend and bring meaning to a text (Prior Knowledge)
- summarize major ideas in a text (Summarize Major Ideas)

Literary Elements: The student will apply knowledge of literary elements to understand written texts. The student will:

- analyze characters from a story (Character Analysis)
- analyze conflict and problem resolution (Conflict/Resolution)
- recognize and interpret literary devices (flashback, foreshadowing, symbolism, simile, metaphor, etc.) (Literary Devices)
- consider characters' points of view (Point of View)
- recognize and analyze a story's setting (Setting)
- understand and explain themes in a text (Theme)

Analyze Written Texts: The student will use a variety of strategies to analyze written texts. The student will:

- identify the author's purpose (Author's Purpose)
- identify cause and effect relationships in a text (Cause/Effect)
- identify characteristics representative of a given genre (Genre)
- interpret information given in a text (Interpret Text)
- make and verify predictions with information from a text (Predictions)
- sequence events in chronological order (Sequencing)
- identify and use multiple text formats (Text Format)
- follow written directions and write directions for others to follow (Follow/Write Directions)

Critical Thinking: The student will apply critical-thinking skills to analyze written texts. The student will:

- write and complete analogies (Analogies)
- find similarities and differences throughout a text (Compare/Contrast)
- draw conclusions from information given (Drawing Conclusions)
- make and explain inferences (Inferences)
- respond to texts by making connections and observations (Making Connections)
- recognize and identify the mood of a text (Mood)
- recognize an author's style and how it affects a text (Style)
- support responses by referring to relevant aspects of a text (Support Responses)
- recognize and identify the author's tone (Tone)
- write to entertain, such as through humorous poetry or short stories (Write to Entertain)
- write to express ideas (Write to Express)
- write to inform (Write to Inform)
- write to persuade (Write to Persuade)
- demonstrate understanding by creating visual images based on text descriptions (Visualizing)
- practice math skills as they relate to a text (Math Skills)

Name ______________________________

Attribute Web

Directions: Brainstorm the meanings and qualities of a good friend, and write them on the spokes of the attribute web.

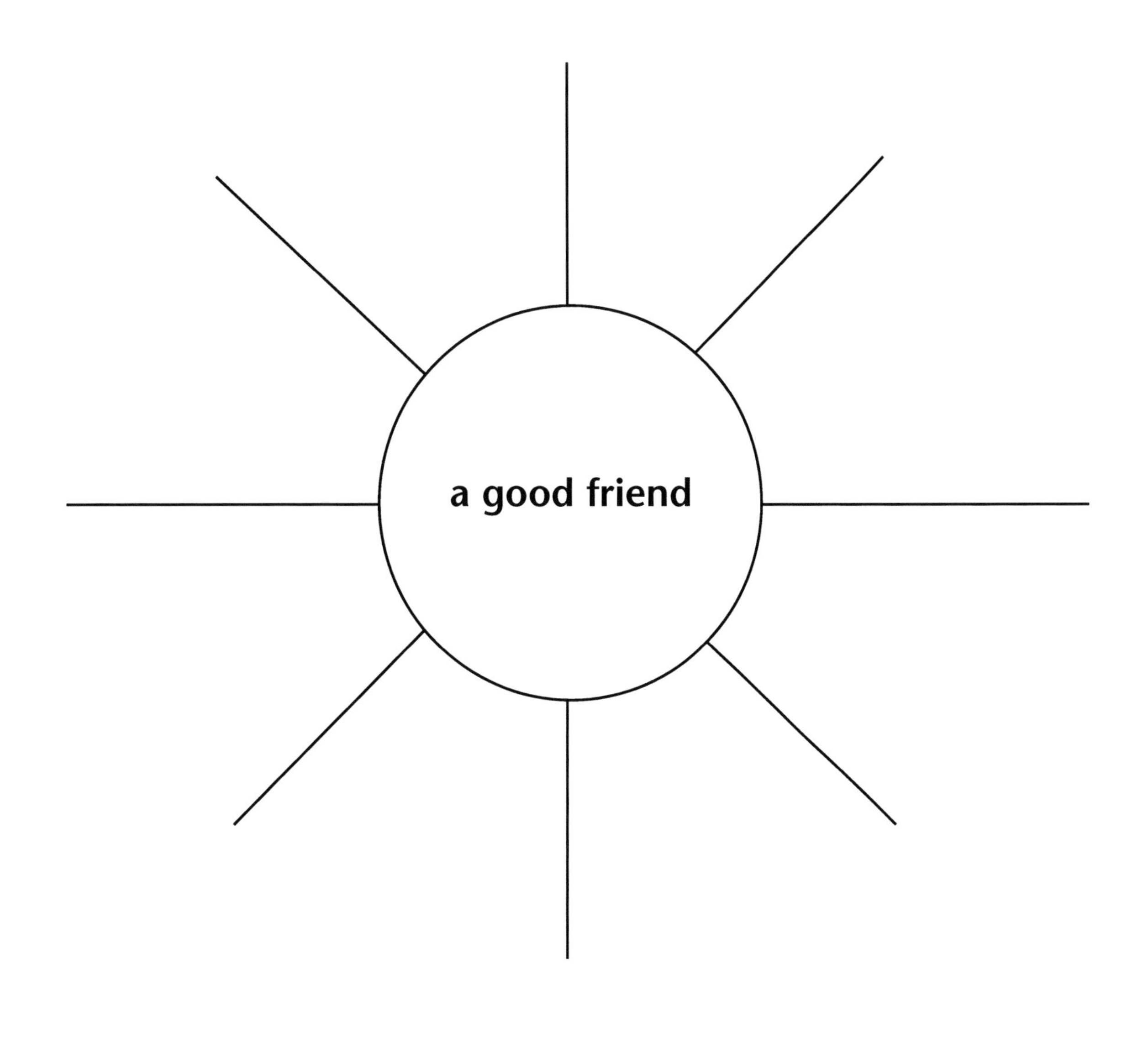

Name ______________________________

Anticipation Guide

Directions: Rate each of the following statements before you read the novel, and discuss your ratings with a partner. After you have completed the novel, rate and discuss the statements again.

1 ———— 2 ———— 3 ———— 4 ———— 5 ———— 6
strongly agree — strongly disagree

	Before	After
1. Jealousy has no place in a friendship.	_____	_____
2. Young people are mostly interested in stories about themselves and their friends.	_____	_____
3. Only visually-impaired people need to learn to read Braille.	_____	_____
4. Cooking is something only adults do.	_____	_____
5. People should rarely express their feelings.	_____	_____
6. We are influenced the most by those closest to us.	_____	_____
7. Sometimes people should apologize even if they don't think they have done anything wrong.	_____	_____
8. It is a good idea to be suspicious of someone or something unfamiliar.	_____	_____
9. We should make friends with people who are similar to us.	_____	_____
10. Sometimes the little things in life are what are most important.	_____	_____

Name ______________________________

Word Map

compliment	spiteful	rooting	snatches
fling	snares	swirling	inseparable
rummaging			

Directions: Complete the chart below for at least five of the vocabulary words listed above.

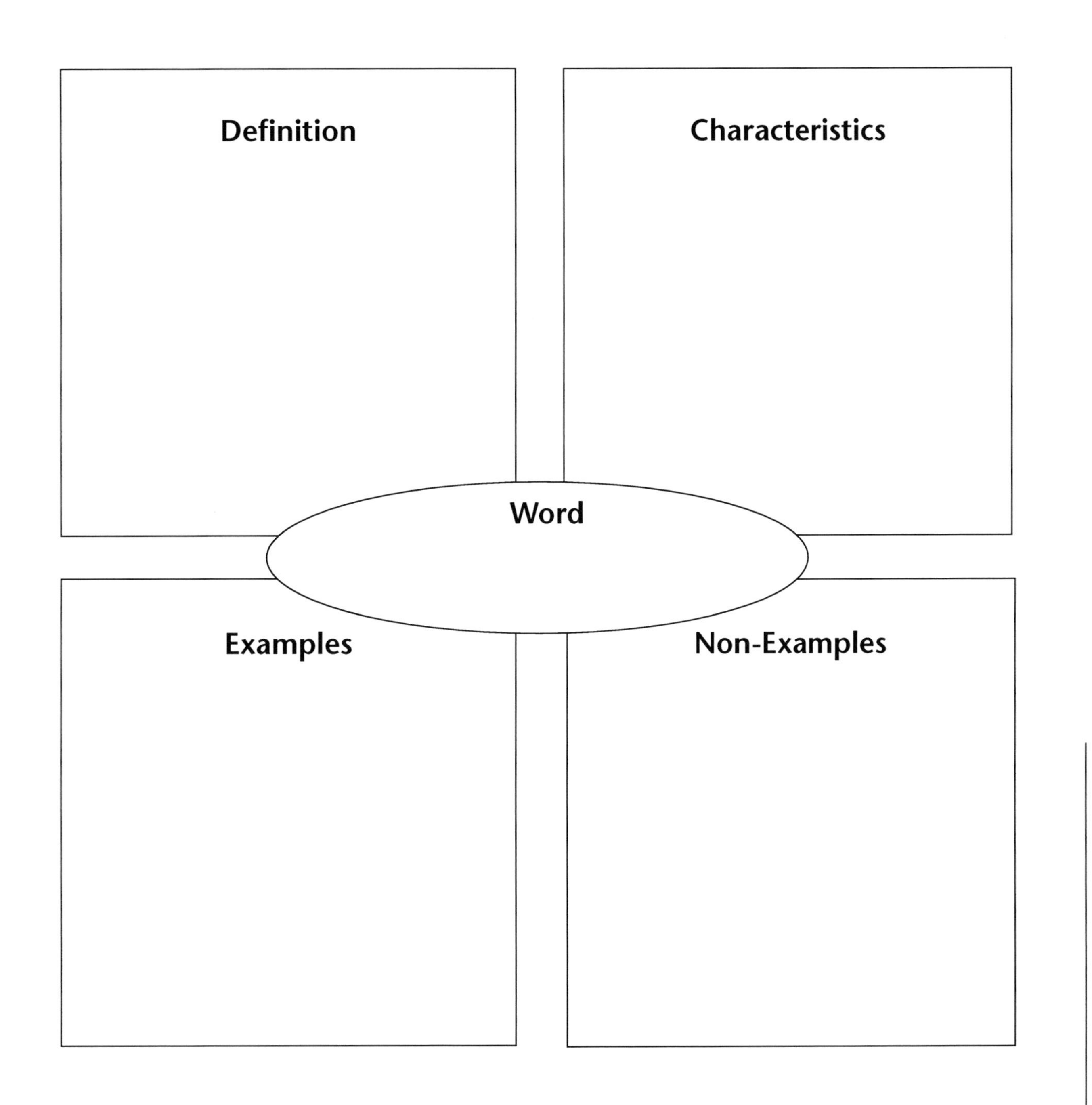

Name ______________________________

Granny Torrelli Makes Soup
Activity #4 • Vocabulary
Soup: Put Your Feet Up–Tangled Head

Vocabulary Board

distracts	mangy	slosh	fetch
loping	prickled	ditto	lured
delicatessen	slurps	straggled	

Directions: Write each vocabulary word on an index card, and place the cards face down by the Vocabulary Board below. Each player rolls a die and moves that many spaces. Then the player draws a word card (if prompted) and follows the directions on the space where s/he lands. If the player answers correctly, s/he remains on that space. If the player answers incorrectly, s/he returns to Start. The game ends when the first player reaches Finish.

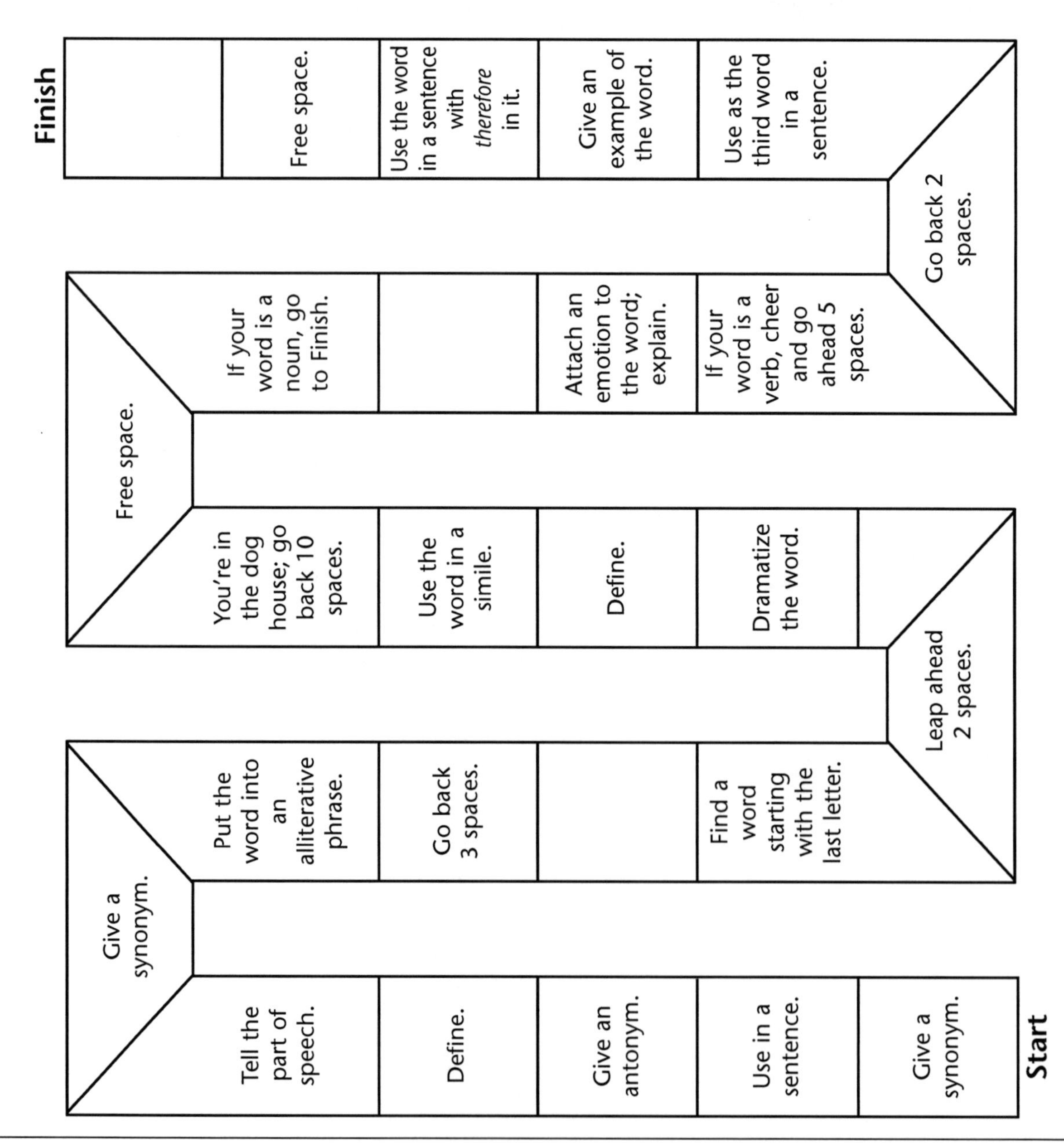

Name ________________________________

Vocabulary Chart

roaming	ghastly	whacking	parsley
flopped	smug	wail	nuisance
dazzling	fare	chattering	

Directions: Write each vocabulary word in the left-hand column of the chart. Complete the chart by placing a check mark in the column that best describes your familiarity with each word. Working with a partner, find and read the line where each word appears in the story. Find the meaning of each word in the dictionary. Together with your partner, choose seven of the words checked in the last column. On a separate sheet of paper, use each of those words in a sentence.

Vocabulary Word	I Can Define	I Have Seen/Heard	New Word For Me

Name ____________________

Word Map

pastry	plucking	sifts	whisking
puckers	flattered	suspended	tilted
mangling	swooned	throttle	

Directions: Complete a word map for at least five of the vocabulary words listed above.

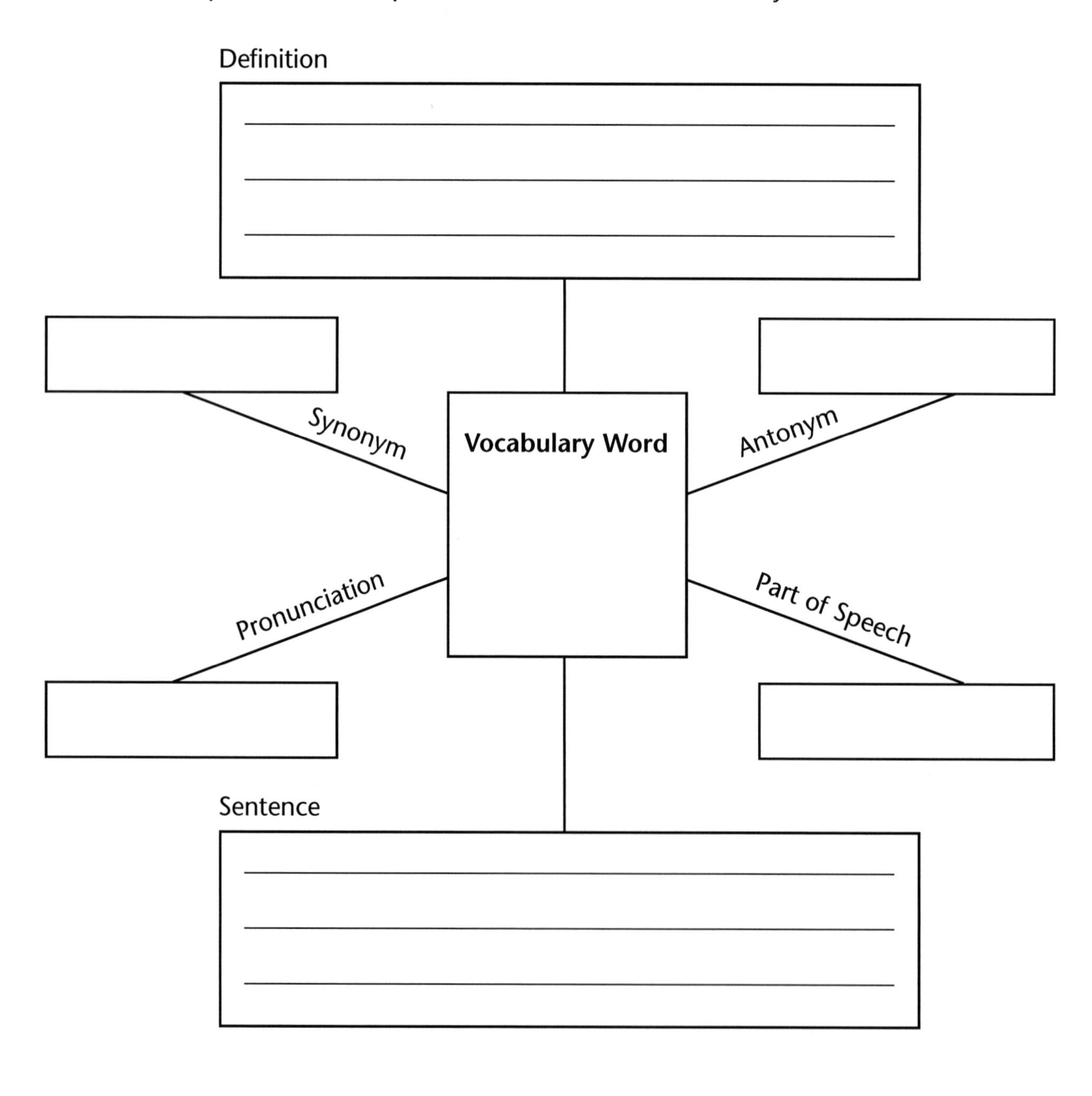

Name ______________________________

Vocabulary Sentence Sets

slink	wretched	heaves	flounder
uttering	kneads	oregano	dribbles
wee	enchanting	flicks	

Directions: Write the vocabulary words from the list above on the numbered lines below.

1. ______________________________ 2. ______________________________
3. ______________________________ 4. ______________________________
5. ______________________________ 6. ______________________________
7. ______________________________ 8. ______________________________
9. ______________________________ 10. ______________________________
11. ______________________________

On a separate sheet of paper, use each of the following sets of words in an original sentence. Your sentences should show that you know the meanings of the vocabulary words as they are used in the story.

Sentence 1: words 8 and 4
Sentence 2: words 9 and 3
Sentence 3: words 1 and 10
Sentence 4: words 11 and 7
Sentence 5: words 3 and 6
Sentence 6: words 2 and 5
Sentence 7: words 1 and 9
Sentence 8: words 10 and 2
Sentence 9: words 4 and 5
Sentence 10: words 8 and 6

Name ______________________________

Vocabulary Mobile

agitated	annoyed	mumbles	assessing
sly	glance	pounce	lullabies
zinnias	awkward		

Directions: Working in groups of five, choose at least five words from the vocabulary list above and make a triangle for each. Cut a nine-inch square out of white construction paper. Fold paper in half diagonally (from corner to corner). Unfold the paper. Fold the paper in half again (Figure A). Then, cut one fold from the outer corner to the center of the paper (Figure B). Slide one cut piece on top of the other to form a triangular shape (resembling a pyramid, but without a base). Glue the pieces together (Figure C). On one side, write a vocabulary word, its definition, a synonym, and an antonym (if applicable). On another side, write a sentence using the vocabulary word. On the third side, draw a picture to illustrate the vocabulary word. All groups should combine their triangles and hang them in the classroom as a mobile.

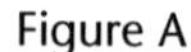

Figure A

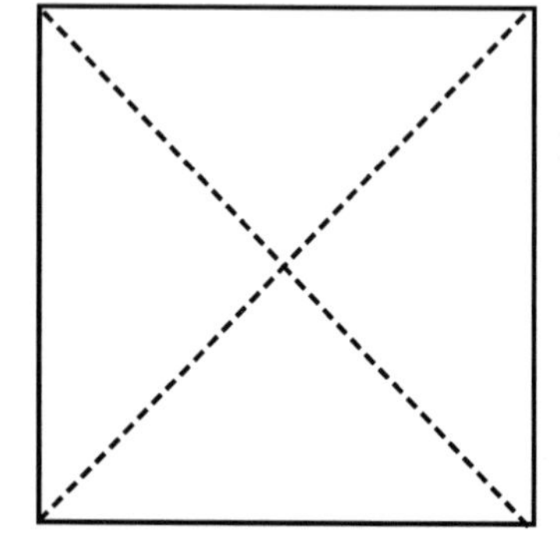

1–Fold in half diagonally

2–Fold in half again

Figure B

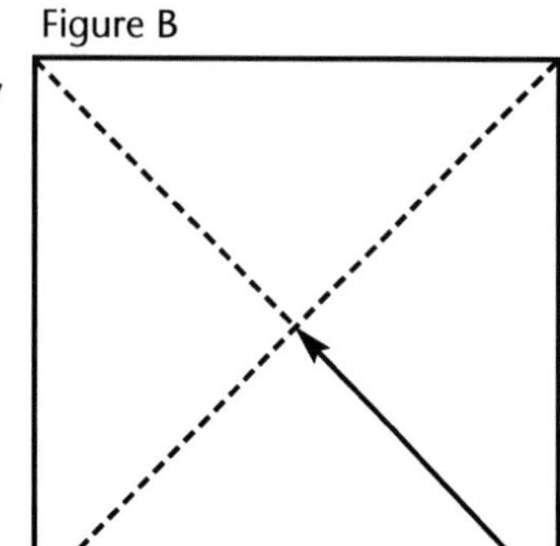

Cut from corner to center in direction of arrow

Figure C

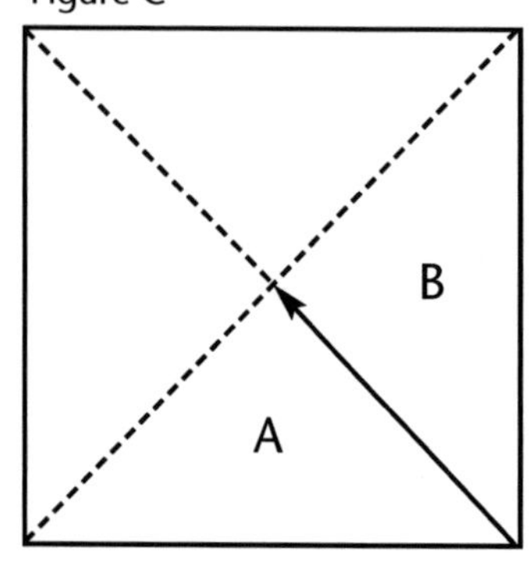

1–Slide one cut piece (A) on top of the other cut piece (B)
2–Glue together to form a triangular shape

Name ______________________________

Directions: Write a brief answer to each question as you read the novel at home or in class. Use the questions to guide your reading, prepare for class discussions, and review for quizzes and tests.

Part I. Soup
That Bailey–Just Like Bailey

1. Where does Bailey live?
2. Describe Granny Torrelli.
3. Why does Rosie like Bailey?
4. Describe Bailey's physical appearance.
5. Describe Bailey's personality.
6. What kind of soup does Granny Torrelli make?
7. What does Granny Torrelli ask Rosie while making soup?
8. Who is Pardo?
9. What upsets Rosie so much when she starts school?
10. How old are Rosie and Bailey?

Put Your Feet Up–Tangled Head

1. What kind of "special stuff" does Bailey have?
2. How does Rosie teach Bailey the alphabet?
3. What roles do Rosie and Bailey take in their plays?
4. What does Pardo have that makes Granny Torrelli jealous when they are children?
5. How does Granny Torrelli plan to make Nero love her?
6. What does Rosie do to try to help Bailey get a guide dog?
7. What goes wrong with Rosie's plan?
8. How does Granny Torrelli describe heaven?
9. How old is Granny Torrelli when she leaves Italy?

Name ______________________________

Lost–*Tutto*

1. Where do Bailey's family and friends find him when they think he is lost?
2. After Bailey punches Rosie, why doesn't she cry?
3. How does Bailey know that the two bullies are attacking Rosie?
4. Why don't the two bullies realize that Bailey has a sight problem?
5. What is the surprise Rosie has for Bailey and her family?
6. What is Bailey's reaction to Rosie's surprise?
7. About what do Pardo and Granny Torrelli disagree?
8. What happened to Pardo?
9. How does Granny Torrelli's story about her lost friendship with Pardo affect Rosie?

Part II. Pasta
She's Back–Violetta

1. When does Granny Torrelli return to visit Rosie?
2. What food does Granny Torrelli make with Rosie and Bailey on this visit?
3. What ingredients are in this recipe?
4. Does Granny Torrelli follow a written recipe? Why or why not?
5. Who has moved into the neighborhood?
6. Why does Rosie feel conflicted upon first meeting Janine?
7. What causes Rosie to feel jealous of Janine?
8. Who is Violetta?
9. Why is Granny Torrelli jealous of Violetta?

Janine–Sauce

1. Who unexpectedly arrives at Rosie's house?
2. Why does Janine come to Rosie's house?
3. Why isn't tomorrow a good time for Janine's lesson?
4. What does Granny Torrelli do to Violetta's hair?
5. How does Granny Torrelli's plan fail?
6. What happens when Bailey asks Rosie if she is jealous of Janine?
7. What are "snakes"?

Name ______________________________

8. What type of pasta noodles are Granny Torrelli, Rosie, and Bailey making? What does Rosie think the noodles look like?
9. Why does Granny Torrelli think that Marco arriving in the neighborhood is a good thing?
10. What does Pardo think of Marco?

The Yellow House–The Pasta Party

1. What does Rosie see at the empty house across from Bailey's house?
2. What does Rosie think when she sees the two boys moving in?
3. What does Rosie tell Bailey that the new boys could teach her?
4. How does Bailey react when Rosie tells him this?
5. What happens to the Gattozzi baby?
6. What does Rosie realize after hearing Granny Torrelli's story about the baby? How does the story make her feel?
7. Who comes to the pasta party?
8. What does Granny Torrelli mean when she says "*Tutto va bene*"?

Name ______________________________

Character Growth

Directions: Characters often "grow" throughout a novel as they learn and change. Write Rosie's name in the center of the tree rings below. In the surrounding rings, write either examples of Rosie's growth or events that cause the growth. Write the examples or events in the order they occurred in the novel.

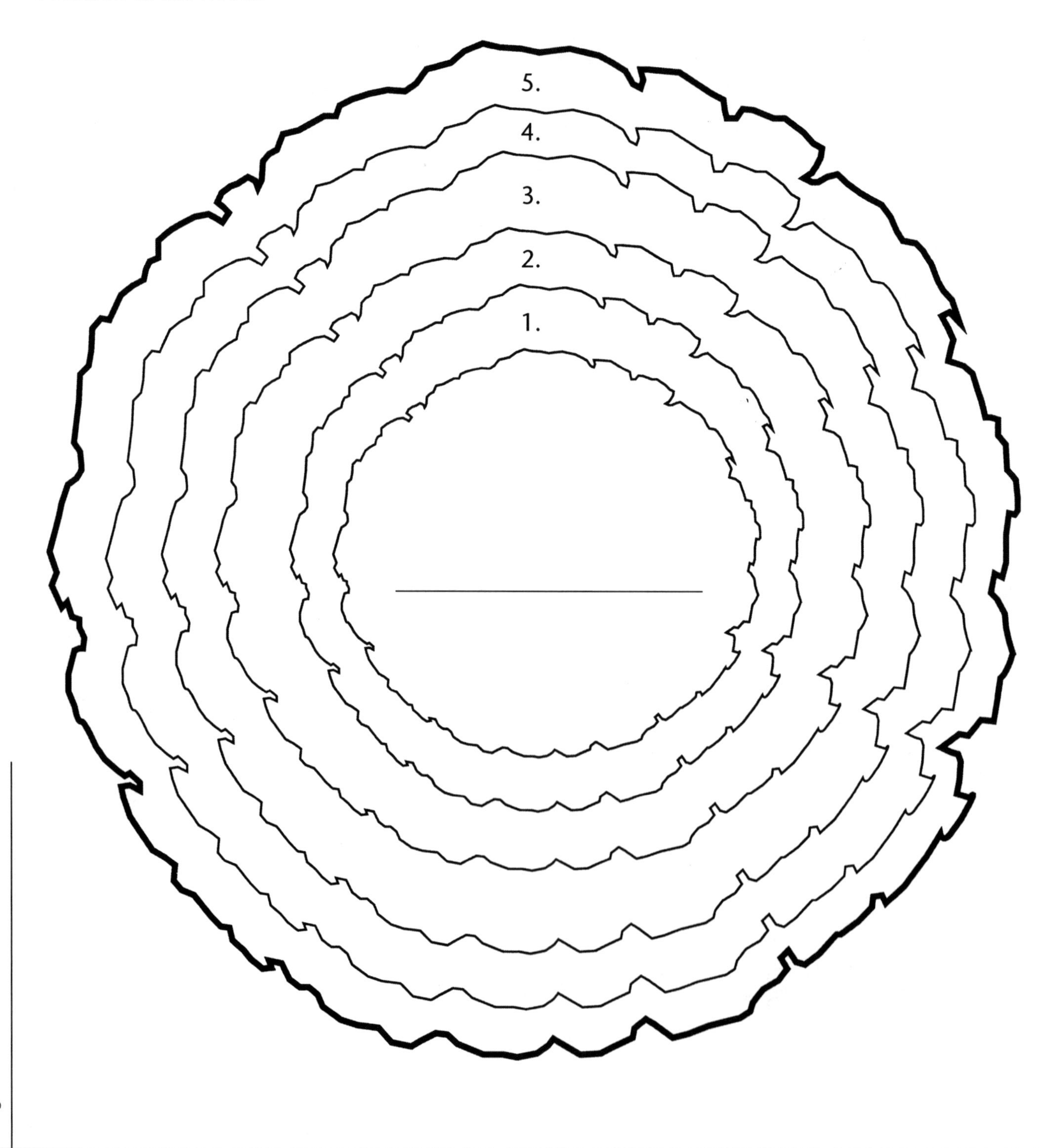

Name ______________________________

Solving Problems

Directions: List six problems the characters in the novel face. Then complete the rest of the chart. For each problem, circle which solution you think is best—yours or the character's.

Problem	Character's Solution	Your Solution

Name ______________________________

Granny Torrelli Makes Soup
Activity #11 • Character Analysis
Use During/After Reading
(Character Analysis)

Feelings

Directions: Choose a character from the book and complete the chart below.

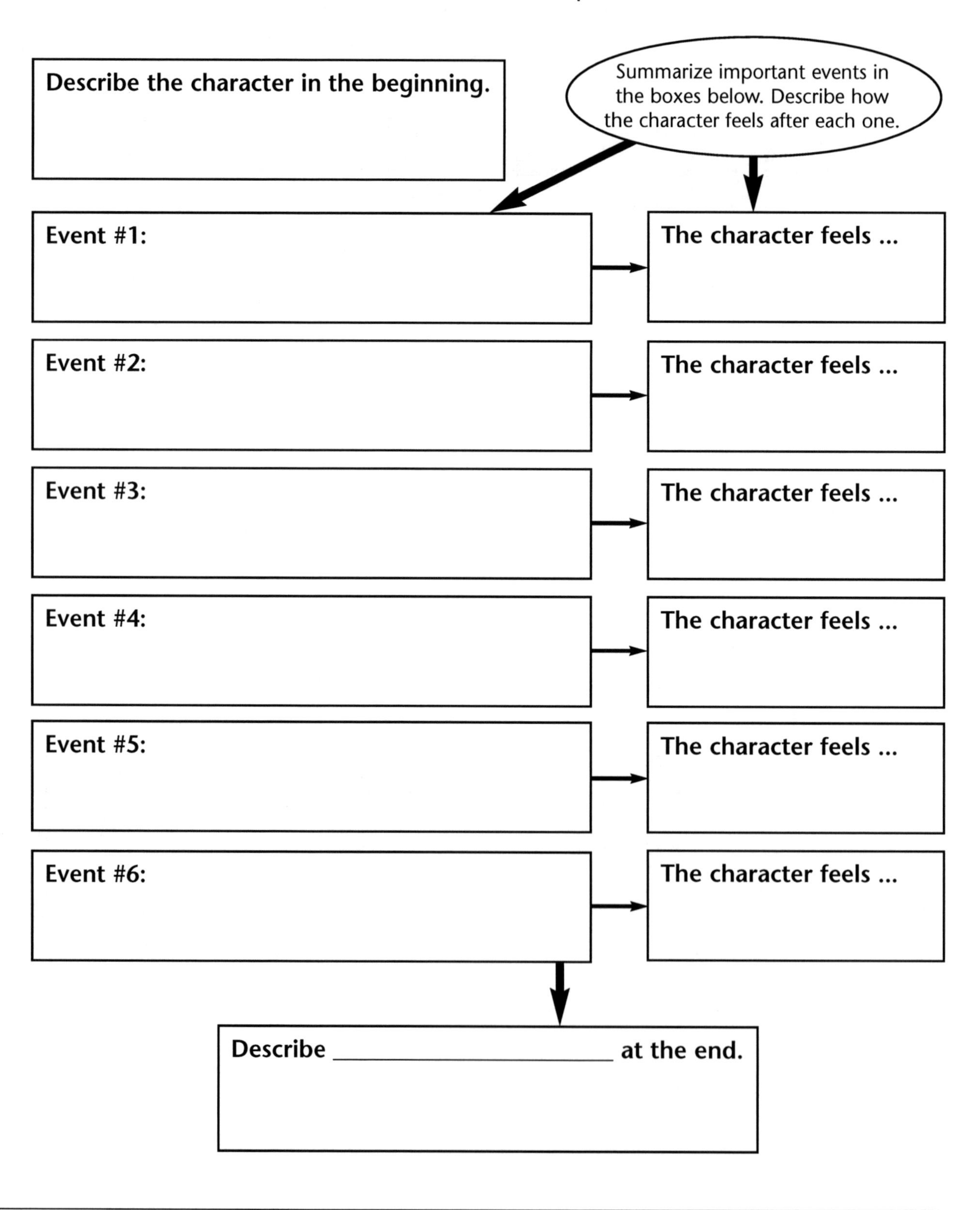

Name ______________________________

Story Map

Directions: Complete the story map for *Granny Torrelli Makes Soup*.

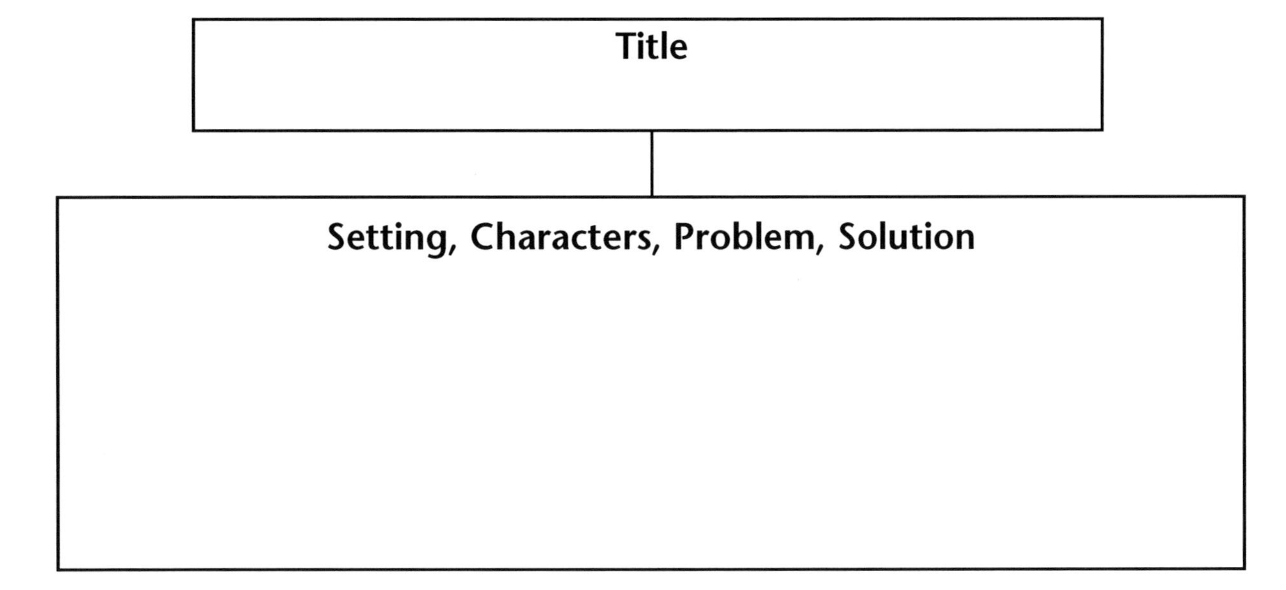

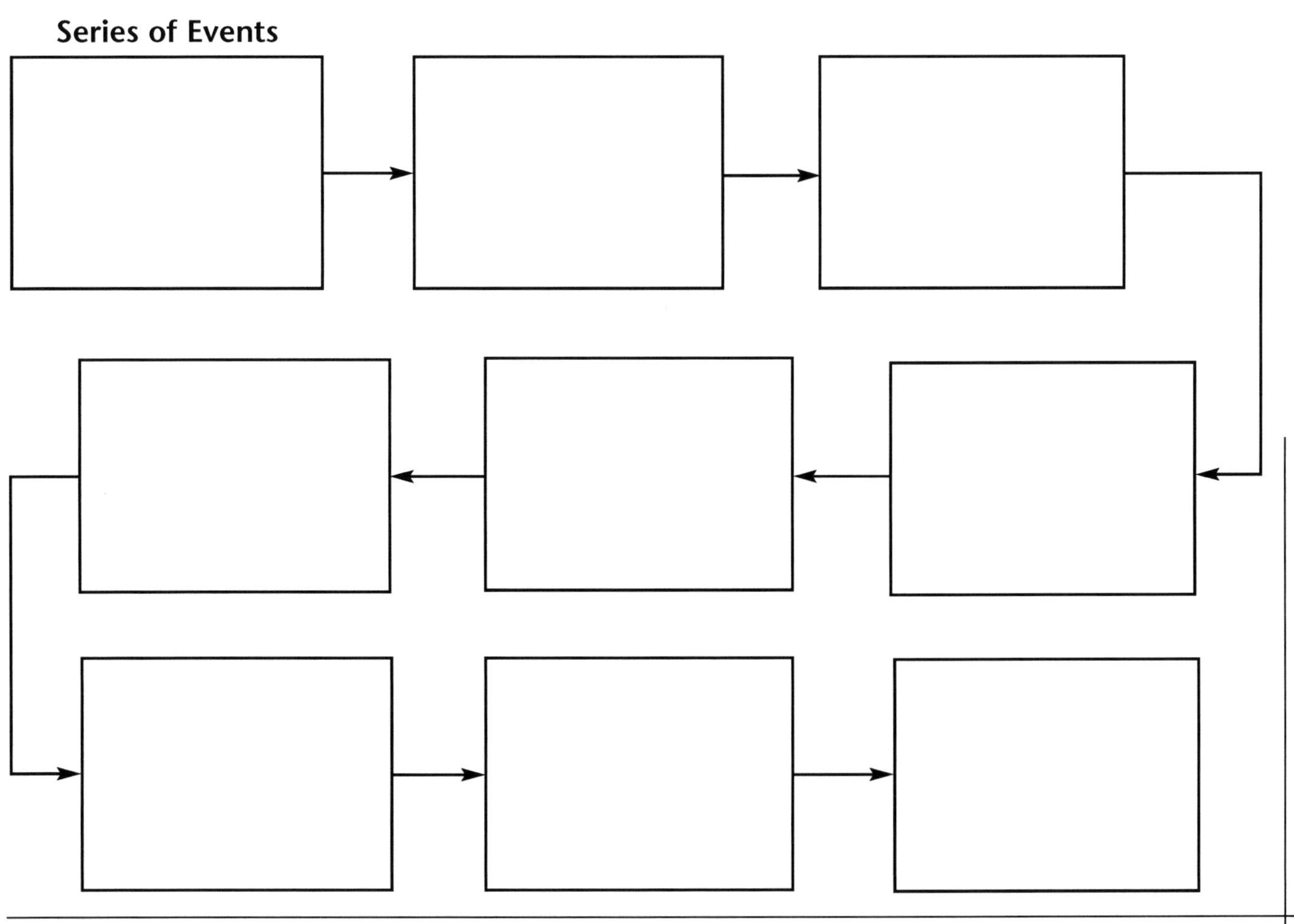

Name ______________________________

Conflict

The **conflict** of a story is the struggle between two people or two forces. There are three main types of conflict: person vs. person, person vs. nature or society, and person vs. self.

Directions: The characters experience some conflicts in the story. In the chart below, list the names of three major characters. In the space provided, list a conflict each character experiences. Then explain how each conflict is resolved in the story.

Character:

Conflict	Resolution

Character:

Conflict	Resolution

Character:

Conflict	Resolution

Name ______________________________

Attribute Web

Directions: Brainstorm the possible causes and effects of jealousy. Write three causes and four effects of jealousy in the boxes of the attribute web below.

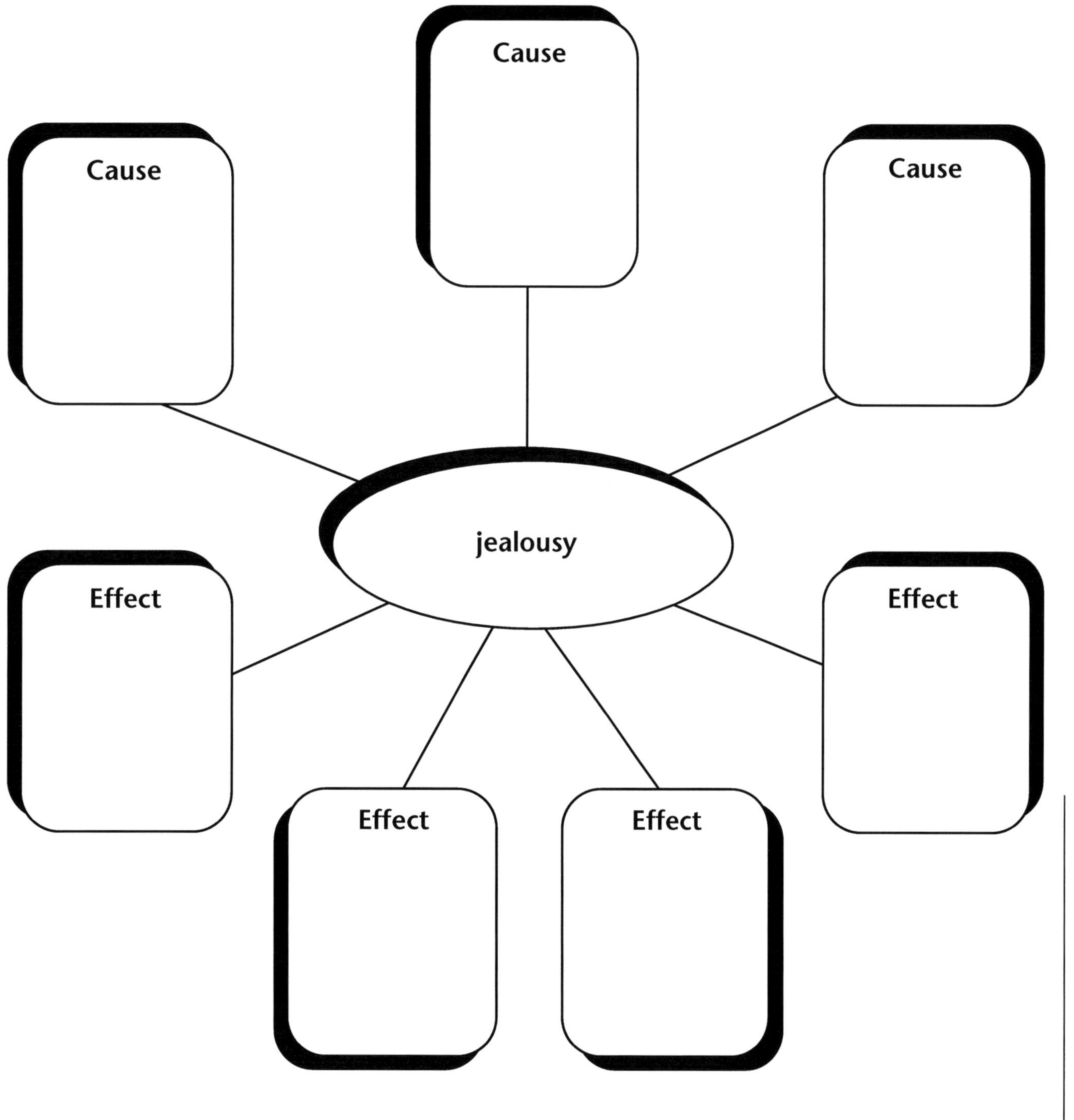

Name ______________________________

Granny Torrelli Makes Soup
Activity #15 • Character Analysis
Use After Reading
(Character Analysis)

Sociogram

Directions: A sociogram shows the relationship between characters in a story. Complete the sociogram below by writing a word to describe the relationships between the characters. Remember, relationships go both ways, so each line requires a descriptive word.

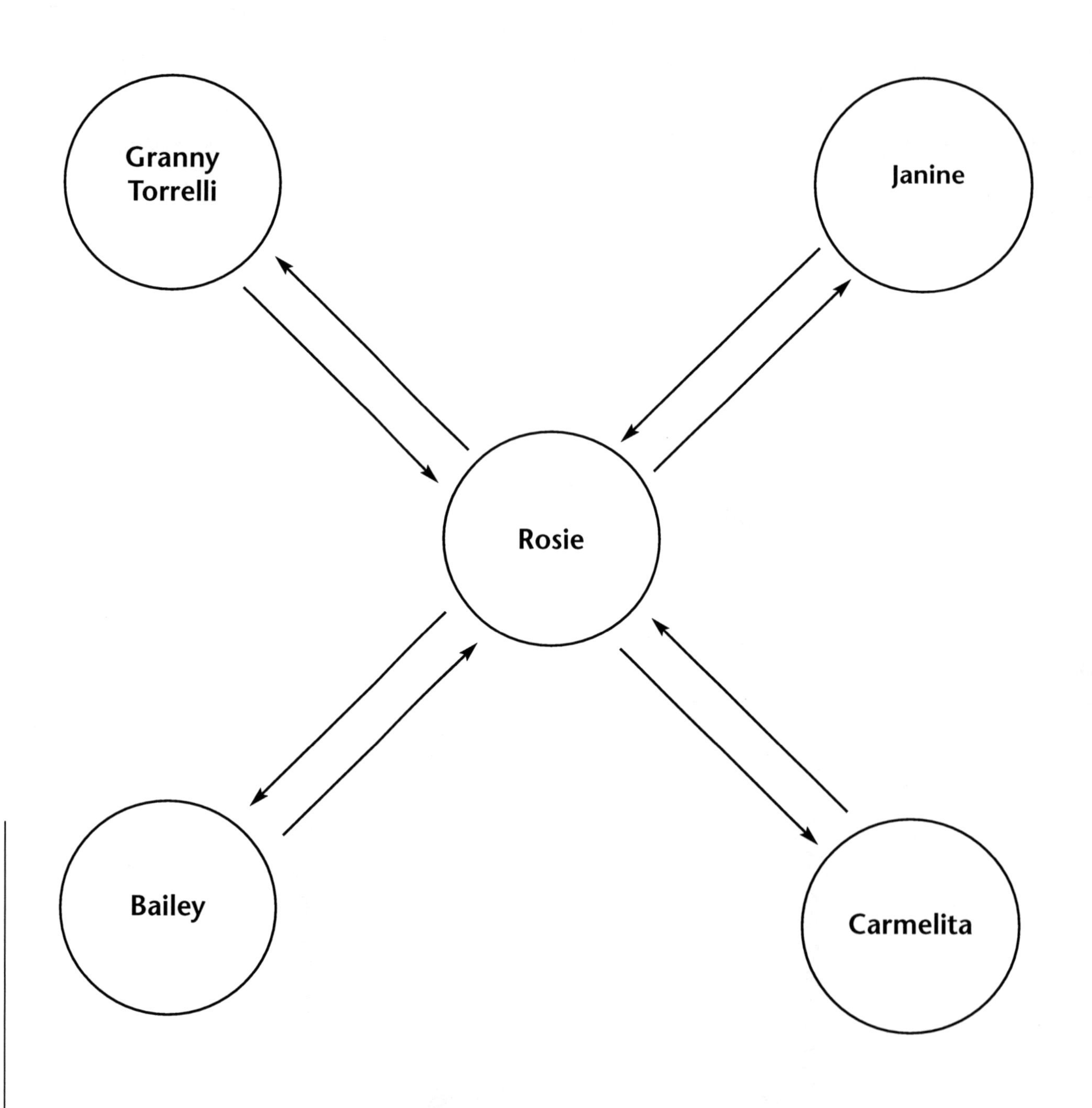

Name ______________________________

(Main Idea and Details)

True/False: Place a *T* beside the statement if it is true and an *F* beside the statement if it is false.

____ 1. Granny Torrelli was born in Italy.

____ 2. Bailey's little brother was born blind.

____ 3. Granny Torrelli is a great cook who always follows recipes exactly.

____ 4. Granny Torrelli and Pardo were childhood best friends.

____ 5. Rosie and Bailey have been best friends since they were born.

____ 6. Rosie and Bailey began school together, but now they go to different schools.

____ 7. Rosie is jealous of Bailey because he can read Braille and she cannot.

____ 8. Granny Torrelli and Rosie make soup for Carmelita's engagement party.

____ 9. Pardo's black cat, Nero, is his best friend.

____ 10. Granny Torrelli thinks she has lost Nero when she takes him to the woods.

____ 11. Rosie tries to train a guide dog for Bailey.

____ 12. *Tutto va bene* is Italian for "All is well."

____ 13. Bailey says that a person must be 16 years old before s/he can get a guide dog.

____ 14. Rosie and Bailey burn the soup when Granny Torrelli goes to the bathroom.

Name ______________________________

Multiple Choice: Choose the BEST answer for each of the following.

(Main Idea and Details)

____ 1. What is the Italian word for "soup"?

a. *bambini*

b. *bene*

c. *piccolino*

d. *zuppa*

(Cause/Effect)

____ 2. How does Bailey know to rescue Rosie from the bullies?

a. He can see them.

b. He can hear them.

c. He can smell their gym socks.

d. He can feel them breathing on his neck.

(Cause/Effect)

____ 3. Why is Rosie is angry with Bailey?

a. Bailey eats all the soup.

b. Bailey is angry with Rosie.

c. Bailey is rude to his mother.

d. Bailey is disrespectful to Granny Torrelli.

(Cause/Effect)

____ 4. Why is Bailey so upset with Rosie?

a. Rosie left Bailey alone in the park.

b. Rosie taught herself to read Braille.

c. Rosie and Janine became best friends.

d. Rosie did not invite him to her school play.

(Main Idea and Details)

____ 5. How old is Granny Torrelli when she comes to America?

a. 12

b. 14

c. 16

d. 18

Name ______________________________

(Main Idea and Details)

____ 6. What happened to Pardo?

a. He died in the war.

b. He became an artist.

c. He was killed on a railroad track.

d. He married Granny Torrelli's best friend.

(Character Analysis)

____ 7. What lesson does Granny Torrelli learn from her friendship with Pardo?

a. Keep your money in a safe place.

b. Don't be too stubborn to say you are sorry.

c. Good friends always share the love of a dog.

d. Always share your soup with someone less fortunate.

(Main Idea and Details)

____ 8. What does Bailey write to Rosie in Braille?

a. "Go home."

b. "I'm sorry."

c. "Keep smiling."

d. "Let's eat."

(Cause/Effect)

____ 9. Why does Rosie call herself an "ice queen"?

a. Janine has invited her to a winter party.

b. She is suspicious of the too-friendly Janine.

c. She is the best ice skater in the neighborhood.

d. She likes to eat ice cream with her soup and pasta.

(Cause/Effect)

____ 10. When does Rosie's "ice queen" turn into a tiger?

a. when she has a fight with a bully

b. when she defends Bailey at school

c. when she thinks Bailey likes Janine more than her

d. when the next-door neighbor insults Granny Torrelli

Name ______________________________

(Main Idea and Details)

Fill in the Blanks: Complete each of the following statements with the correct word(s).

1. ________________ asks Bailey to give her _______________ lessons.
2. ________________ cuts Violetta's hair to ______________________.
3. Pardo thinks Violetta looks like a ________________________.
4. Rosie is ________________ of Janine because she thinks ________________ likes Janine better.
5. Granny Torrelli's rolled pasta looks like _____________, and the shaped cavatelli noodles look like ________________.
6. ______________ finds Granny enchanting.
7. The new neighbors have one _____________ and two ________________.
8. Bailey is ______________ because Rosie suggests that the neighbor boys could teach her how to play ___________________.
9. The Gattozzi baby is very ___________, and _______________ is frightened.
10. Rosie invites Janine and the new neighbors to the __________________.

Name ______________________________

(Character Analysis)
A. Matching: Match each character with his/her action. Some characters may be used more than once.

____ 1. asks Bailey to teach her how to read Braille
____ 2. wants to get a guide dog for Bailey
____ 3. allows Granny Torrelli to cut her hair
____ 4. is a good listener
____ 5. wants Granny Torrelli to stay in Italy
____ 6. learns to read Braille in secret
____ 7. describes herself as a "monster"
____ 8. finds Granny Torrelli enchanting
____ 9. describes herself as an "ice queen"
____10. searches for a lost dog in the woods

a. Granny Torrelli
b. Rosie
c. Bailey
d. Janine
e. Pardo
f. Violetta
g. Marco

(Literary Devices)
B. Flashback: Place an *F* in front of the events from the novel that are told using the literary device of flashback.

____11. Granny Torrelli and Rosie make chicken soup.
____12. Granny Torrelli and Pardo are best friends.
____13. Rosie cries when Bailey must go to a different school.
____14. Granny Torrelli asks Rosie why she is upset with Bailey.
____15. Granny Torrelli is jealous of Nero.
____16. Rosie tries to train Tootie to be a guide dog.
____17. Bailey defends Rosie against two bullies.
____18. Rosie reads Braille to Bailey.
____19. Granny Torrelli is angry with herself for not apologizing to Pardo.
____20. Bailey helps Granny Torrelli and Rosie make pasta.
____21. Janine asks Rosie to be her best girl friend.
____22. Pardo is infatuated with Violetta.
____23. The Jefferson family joins their new neighbors for a pasta party.

Name ______________________________

(Cause/Effect)

C. Short Answer: Write a brief answer for each of the following. You may use a separate sheet of paper if necessary.

24. Why is Bailey unhappy that Rosie learns to read Braille?

____

____

25. Why is Granny Torrelli sad when she thinks of Pardo?

____

____

26. Why does Rosie say she turns from an "ice queen" to a tiger?

____

____

27. Why isn't Rosie upset when Bailey punches her after she tells him he was lost?

____

____

28. How does Bailey tell Rosie that he is sorry?

____

____

29. Why is Rosie so angry with Janine?

____

____

30. Why is Rosie furious that Bailey offers to teach Janine to read Braille?

____

____

31. Why does Granny Torrelli tell stories of Pardo and Violetta to Rosie and Bailey?

____

____

Name ______________________________

D. Essay: Choose one of the following and write a well-developed, 2- to 3-paragraph essay on the lines below. Cite specific evidence from the novel and class discussions to support your response. You may use a separate sheet of paper if necessary.

(Compare/Contrast)

a. Compare and contrast the main characters in the novel with the characters from Granny Torrelli's stories. Which of the characters are most alike? most different?

(Making Connections)

b. Choose two of the life lessons recorded in your journal. Describe a time in which you applied these lessons to your own life. How did you benefit from the lessons?

(Literary Devices)

c. Much of the novel is told using flashback. Choose an event presented in this format, and explain how it is effective in advancing the plot of the novel.

____

____

____

____

____

____

____

____

____

____

____

____

____

____

Answer Key

Activity #1: Answers will vary. Suggestions—honest, loyal, trustworthy, kind, supportive, fun-loving, sense of humor, cooperative

Activities #2–#3: Answers will vary.

Activity #4: Students will play the Vocabulary Board game.

Activities #5–#8: Answers will vary.

Study Guide
Part I. Soup: That Bailey–Just Like Bailey: 1. next door to Rosie 2. reasonable, calm, patient, brave, good cook 3. They were born one week apart and have lived next door to each other their entire lives. They do everything together. 4. He has freckles, smiles a lot, and has soft hair that sticks up. 5. He is unselfish, not pushy, not mean (usually), and quiet (sometimes). 6. chicken soup with vegetables 7. why she is so sad about Bailey 8. Granny Torrelli's childhood friend 9. Bailey does not go to the same school as her. 10. 12 years old

Put Your Feet Up–Tangled Head: 1. recorded books and Braille books 2. She writes the letters with fat, black markers. 3. mother and father or sister and brother 4. a mangy black dog named Nero 5. by taking Nero for a walk in the woods and giving him little chocolates 6. She takes in a "stray dog," hides it in the garage, and tries to teach it to obey commands. 7. The dog will not obey Rosie, and then the dog's owner hears the dog barking in Rosie's garage. 8. as a big pasta party 9. 16 years old

Lost–*Tutto*: 1. on his front porch eating a peanut butter and jelly sandwich 2. She is glad that he wasn't lost and that terrible things did not happen to him. 3. He hears them. 4. Bailey is wearing sunglasses, and they cannot see his eyes. 5. She has secretly learned to read Braille. 6. He is extremely upset, accuses her of cheating, and slams the door behind her as she leaves. 7. Pardo wants Granny to marry him and stay in Italy; Granny wants to go to America and have adventures. 8. He was killed by a train while trying to rescue his dog, which was trapped on a railroad track. 9. It makes her realize that Bailey is her very best friend, and she does not want to lose his friendship just because she won't apologize.

Part II. Pasta: She's Back–Violetta: 1. one week later on Saturday 2. pasta 3. flour, salt, and eggs 4. no, because Granny Torrelli has made pasta so many times before that she knows how to do so without a recipe 5. Janine 6. Janine wants to be Rosie's best girl friend. 7. Janine asks Bailey to teach her to read Braille, and he agrees without getting upset. 8. a girl who moves to Italy and lives next door to Pardo 9. Granny thinks Violetta is being too nice to Pardo and will take away her best friend.

Janine–Sauce: 1. Janine 2. Janine is looking for Bailey to find out what time to come for her first Braille lesson. 3. Rosie has planned a pasta party for tomorrow, and Bailey and his mom are invited. 4. Granny cuts Violetta's hair, hoping it will make Pardo think she is ugly. 5. Pardo thinks Violetta looks like a movie star with her new haircut. 6. Rosie asks Bailey if he could like Janine better than her and does not like his answer, that "[he doesn't] think so" (p. 111). 7. rolled-out pieces of pasta dough 8. cavatelli; like little dough canoes 9. Marco thinks that Granny Torrelli is "enchanting," and Granny hopes this will make Pardo jealous. 10. Pardo hates Marco.

The Yellow House–The Pasta Party: 1. a moving van, two cars, a man and woman, a little girl, and two boys about her age who might be twins 2. Rosie sees an opportunity to make Bailey jealous if the two boys pay attention to her. 3. how to play basketball 4. He becomes distant, short in his answers, and appears to be angry. 5. The baby gets very sick, and Granny gets very attached to it. She is afraid the baby has died, but it lives. 6. Rosie realizes that life is bigger than she thought, and she cannot control everything. She is happy and relieved. 7. Granny Torrelli, Rosie and her parents, Carmelita and

Bailey, Janine, Mr. and Mrs. Jefferson with their daughter Lucille and their sons Johnny and Jack 8. All is well with Rosie and her friend, Bailey.

Note: Answers to Activities #9–#15 will vary. Suggested answers have been given where applicable.

Activity #9: Suggestions—1. Bailey is unable to begin school with Rosie; Rosie understands that Bailey is different and has special needs. 2. Bailey is angry with Rosie when she learns to read Braille; Rosie realizes that Bailey will not always be proud of the things she does (although she doesn't understand why at this point). 3. Janine moves into the neighborhood; Rosie is aware of how much she likes Bailey and of her need to protect their relationship from outsiders. 4. A new family moves into the neighborhood, and it includes twin boys about Rosie and Bailey's age; Rosie contemplates how to "turn the tables" on Bailey by making him jealous. 5. Granny Torrelli tells the story of the ill Gattozzi baby; Rosie realizes that the world is much larger than she had thought, and she is not the only person that matters.

Activity #10: Answers will vary.

Activity #11: Suggestions for Rosie: Beginning—angry, confused; Event #1—Bailey yells at her after discovering she can read Braille; Rosie feels upset and confused; Event #2—(flashback) Bailey is unable to begin school with her; Rosie feels sad and lonely; Event #3—Janine moves into the neighborhood; Rosie feels suspicious and flattered; Event #4—Bailey agrees to teach Janine to read Braille; Rosie feels angry and jealous; Event #5—Two boys about Rosie's age move into the neighborhood; Rosie feels conniving and excited; Event #6—Granny Torrelli tells the story about the Gattozzi baby being ill; Rosie feels sad and aware of her inability to control things; End—Rosie is happy with her life and able to "share" Bailey with others, knowing that their friendship will remain strong.

Activity #12: Title—*Granny Torrelli Makes Soup*; Setting—Rosie's family's kitchen; Characters—Rosie, Granny Torrelli, Bailey, Janine, Pardo, Violetta; Problem—Bailey is mad at Rosie for learning to read Braille, and Rosie is jealous of Janine, who has stolen Bailey's attention; Solution—Upon hearing Granny Torrelli's various stories, Rosie and Bailey realize how important their friendship is, and Rosie understands that Janine cannot come between them as long as they are such good friends; Series of Events—Answers will vary.

Activity #13: Suggestions: Character—Rosie; Conflict—person vs. person: Rosie and Bailey are angry with each other after Bailey reacts badly to Rosie learning to read Braille; Resolution—Rosie and Bailey realize how much they need each other, and they apologize to each other. Character—Granny Torrelli; Conflict—person vs. person: Granny Torrelli is angry with Violetta for paying so much attention to Pardo and angry at Pardo for finding Violetta attractive; Resolution—Granny Torrelli cuts Violetta's hair (attempted)/Marco moves into the neighborhood, and Pardo is jealous (actual). Character—Bailey; Conflict—person vs. nature: Bailey is visually impaired; Resolution: There is none, although Bailey goes to a special school, learns how to do some things using his hands and sense of hearing, and reads Braille to be able to function in society.

Activity #14: Answers will vary.

Activity #15: Rosie and Granny Torrelli—dependent, loving; Rosie and Bailey—protective, appreciative; Rosie and Janine—suspicious, friendly; Rosie and Carmelita—helpful, grateful

Quiz #1: 1. T 2. F 3. F 4. T 5. T 6. F 7. T 8. F 9. F 10. T 11. T 12. T 13. T 14. F

Quiz #2: 1. d 2. b 3. b 4. b 5. c 6. c 7. b 8. b 9. b 10. c

Quiz #3: 1. Janine; Braille 2. Granny Torrelli; make her look ugly 3. movie star 4. jealous; Bailey 5. snakes; canoes 6. Marco 7. daughter; sons 8. jealous OR angry; basketball 9. sick; Granny Torrelli 10. pasta party

Novel Test: A. 1. d 2. b 3. f 4. a 5. e 6. b 7. a 8. g 9. b 10. a **B.** Items that should be marked with an "F": 12, 13, 15, 16, 17, 22 **C.** 24. It is one thing he could do that she could not, and he no longer feels special. 25. She is angry with herself for being stubborn and not apologizing to Pardo before he died. 26. She is cold and ignores Bailey when Janine is mentioned but turns as aggressive as a tiger when she thinks he might like Janine better than her. 27. She is happy that nothing bad happened to him and that he really is not helpless and can find his way home. 28. He gives her a note written in Braille. 29. Rosie thinks Janine will try to take Bailey away from her. 30. Rosie learned to read Braille, and it upset Bailey. Now he is offering to teach Braille to Janine. 31. Elements of Granny Torrelli's stories mirror what is happening between Rosie and Bailey, and she hopes they will learn lessons from them. **D.** Answers will vary. Refer to the scoring rubric on page 31 of this guide.

Linking Novel Units® Student Packets to National and State Reading Assessments

During the past several years, an increasing number of students have faced some form of state-mandated competency testing in reading. Many states now administer state-developed assessments to measure the skills and knowledge emphasized in their particular reading curriculum. This Novel Units® guide includes open-ended comprehension questions that correlate with state-mandated reading assessments. The rubric below provides important information for evaluating responses to open-ended comprehension questions. Teachers may also use scoring rubrics provided for their own state's competency test.

Scoring Rubric for Open-Ended Items

3-Exemplary	Thorough, complete ideas/information Clear organization throughout Logical reasoning/conclusions Thorough understanding of reading task Accurate, complete response
2-Sufficient	Many relevant ideas/pieces of information Clear organization throughout most of response Minor problems in logical reasoning/conclusions General understanding of reading task Generally accurate and complete response
1-Partially Sufficient	Minimally relevant ideas/information Obvious gaps in organization Obvious problems in logical reasoning/conclusions Minimal understanding of reading task Inaccuracies/incomplete response
0-Insufficient	Irrelevant ideas/information No coherent organization Major problems in logical reasoning/conclusions Little or no understanding of reading task Generally inaccurate/incomplete response

Notes

